Make it Happen

A Journal to Identify and Actualize Your Goals

ANGELA HOOKS

PETER PAUPER PRESS, INC.

WHITE PLAINS, NEW YORK

PETER PAUPER PRESS
Fine Books and Gifts Since 1928

OUR COMPANY

In 1928, at the age of twenty-two, Peter Beilenson began printing books on a small press in the basement of his parents' home in Larchmont, New York. Peter—and later, his wife, Edna—sought to create fine books that sold at "prices even a pauper could afford."

Today, still family owned and operated, Peter Pauper Press continues to honor our founders' legacy—and our customers' expectations—of beauty, quality, and value.

Designed by Heather Zschock

Images used under license from Shutterstock.com

Visit us at www.peterpauper.com

A Journal to Identify and Actualize Your Goals

ANGELA HOOKS

Contents

Introduction

Make It Happen is a step-by-step guide that will inspire you to actualize your goal(s), and provide you with the tools to make it happen. A goal can be anything, big or small. It might be an improvement to any area of your life: financial, career, personal, emotional, health, or spiritual.

You've probably been on this path before. Maybe you've stepped off the path, stopped along the way, or chosen another direction. It's possible you're speculating with "ifs, ands, and buts" or "shoulda, coulda, woulda."

Or maybe you're at a proverbial fork in the road, wondering what to do next. You're living someone else's dream for your life, or living someone else's life, not the one you imagined. You know you're in school to be an engineer because your father and grandfather are engineers. But in your heart, you love playing the piano and want to be a musician.

Or perhaps you've never pursued an ambitious goal before. You've dreamt of fulfillment, doing something that makes your heart sing. But you haven't taken the next step because of these three words: "I'm too busy."

Whatever the case, **Make It Happen** offers seven steps to inspire you on your journey. There's no right or wrong way to follow the steps. You can take one or two steps at a time. You can start in the middle or at the end, and then begin again.

Each section begins with a narrative, followed by A STEP ON THE JOURNEY, a quote, and a few journaling prompts to encourage you on your path. The prompts invite you to dream, to write, to take action, and to reflect. There will be lots of lists. Lists are helpful. They keep you organized, serve as memory aids, help you avoid distractions, and act as motivational tools.

The first step is always to write it down. Get your goals out of your head and onto the page. When you write things down, you create a map that will guide you from where you are to where you want to be. You remember and reflect, you think and coordinate, you get organized. According to Dr. Henriette Anne Klauser, "Putting it on paper alerts part of the brain known as the reticular activating system." The RAS awakens the brain and acts like a filter. Things that matter start to appear.

When you put pen to paper with authenticity and intention, something opens up. The words spill onto the page. Activity in one area generates movement in another. Your brain begins to play. You dream. You see your vision and focus on what matters most to you. You set goals and press forward intentionally despite obstacles in your path. You become fearless, fueled by grit and determination. You trust yourself as your confidence grows, one step at a time. And when your confidence grows, your goal sprouts like a seed. Then you wait for it and learn to reward each part of your success on the journey. Most importantly, you learn to define your own success.

So, let's make it happen!

Explore Your Dreams

Dreams are planted in your heart.

CHAPTER 1

Starting Out

Dare to Dream

When you dare to dream, you explore things beyond your imagination. You focus like a laser beam. Dreams shape not only your life but the lives of those around you.

As a teenager, Kalpana Chawla desired to know all the "nuts and bolts" of aerospace engineering. At the time, the majority of women in India could not read. Because she dared to dream, she became the first woman in the aerospace engineering department of Punjab Engineering College, despite her father's wishes. Years later, Chawla became the first Indian-born woman in space, on the Columbia. Her dream turned into reality and shaped the future dreams of young girls in India.

Humans are created to dream. Dreams are planted in our hearts. They inspire us to reach beyond our ordinary capabilities, and challenge us to move out of our comfort zone. Without dreams we can become restless and unproductive. Pay attention to the longings in your heart. Do you want to be a rock star or win the Nobel Peace Prize? Own a bakery or develop an app? Buy a house or a car? What area in your life do you want to focus on? Listen to the still small voice that stirs you up and creates bubbles of excitement.

Take a minute or two to envision your dream, and dream big.

Put your dream into action.

Let your dream soar beyond your imagination.

An Invitation to Dream

Let's start by exploring these questions.

What were your childhood dreams?

....

....

....

....

What were your high school dreams?

....

....

....

....

What were your early adult dreams?

....

....

....

....

....

What are your dreams now?

What is your greatest dream of all?

Describe it, and write down your feelings about it.

Explore your dream.

What happens in the space between your dream and reality? How can you move out of your routine to make room for your dream?

What are you working on most in your life right now? Where are your energy and effort focused?

_____

_____

_____

_____

_____

_____

_____

_____

Is it part of your dream?

_____

_____

_____

_____

_____

_____

_____

_____

Does it make you happy?

_____

_____

_____

_____

_____

_____

Does it give you confidence?

_____

_____

_____

_____

_____

_____

Does it benefit others?

_____

_____

_____

_____

_____

_____

What would you do with
more...

time?

energy?

money?

....

....

....

....

....

....

....

space?

....

....

....

....

....

....

....

education?

_____

_____

_____

_____

_____

_____

_____

community connection?

_____

_____

_____

_____

_____

_____

_____

encouragement and support?

_____
_____
_____
_____
_____
_____

What would you do if you weren't afraid?

_____
_____
_____
_____
_____
_____

Now is the time to understand more, so that we may fear less.

-Marie Curie

Set a timer and write about your dream for ten to twenty minutes.

Write in faith. Although you may not know the how-to of your process, trust your vision and take small steps.

22

What do you like about your vision?

_____
_____
_____
_____
_____
_____
_____
_____

What scares you?

_____
_____
_____
_____
_____
_____
_____
_____

If you're thinking about it, why not take the risk, and the next logical or not-so-logical step, and make it happen?

The path from Dreams to Success does exist.

May you have the vision to find it, the courage to get on to it, and the perseverance to follow it.

—Kalpana Chawla

Explore. Dream. Discover.

In this space, create a **VISION BOARD** to explore, imagine, and discover your dream. Your vision board will help you take action, make decisions, set goals, create structure, and see growth. Use magazine clippings, photos, and your favorite motivational quotes to help you visualize.

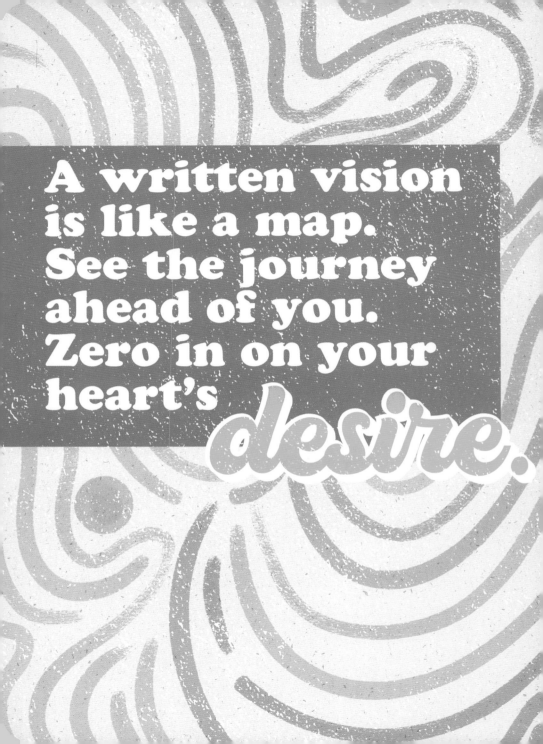

A written vision is like a map. See the journey ahead of you. Zero in on your heart's *desire.*

CHAPTER 2

Making a Commitment

Write Your Vision

Writing is risky. When you write down your vision, you make a commitment to yourself, so your dream doesn't dry up. A written vision is like a map: It gives you a specific direction on your journey. You intentionally set goals. Setting one goal at a time points you to people, places, and resources that will support your dream coming alive. Yes, you will encounter obstacles and challenges, but you must push through. How? Write your vision down. Keep it simple. Write it in one sentence. Write it using the present tense as if it is already true. For example, on the back of one of famous novelist Octavia Butler's notebooks, she wrote: "I shall be a bestselling writer." Then she wrote: "I write bestselling novels."

What about you?
What will you do?

Who are you, and what do you know about yourself?

I am ...

I do ...

I will be ...

Write your vision here.

Keep it simple. Write it using the present tense, as if it is already true.

Writing down your vision takes time and revision. As you grow, your vision grows. You may have to rewrite your vision several times. Each time you revise, it becomes clearer. Writing brings clarity.

Questions to keep asking yourself:

What do you need to get closer to your vision?

What are you good at?

What do people come to you for? What do they repeatedly ask of you?

Does it feel good and/or right to be asked for this?

What do you want to achieve?

_____

_____

_____

_____

_____

_____

_____

_____

_____

_____

_____

_____

_____

_____

_____

Ask yourself these questions again and again, whenever you
need direction, and write the answers down.

...*just*
pay attention, then patch
a few words together and don't try
to make them elaborate, this isn't
a contest but the doorway.

—Mary Oliver, *Praying*

Pay attention to:

YOUR SKILLS, the things you have learned
YOUR STRENGTHS, the things you're naturally good at

Here's a list. Circle at least two of your skills. Underline the ones you want to develop.

Skills

Fluent in more than one language
Clear communicator
Great cook
Detail-oriented
Skilled writer
Graphic designer
Fitness expert
Organized
Can play a musical instrument
Self-motivated
Compelling public speaker
Good teacher
Other:

Now circle at least two of your strengths. Underline the ones you want to develop.

Artistic
Cheerful
Creative
Disciplined
Dedicated
Friendly
Generous
Helpful
Inspirational
Outgoing
Practical
Resourceful
Spiritual
Other:

How can the skills and strengths you have serve your vision?

How can you work on the skills and strengths you hope to acquire?

Vision

is a picture of the future that produces passion.

–Bill Hybels

SEE IT!
SAY IT!
Believe it!

Your vision statement outlines your priorities, and creates goals based on them.

Since your vision statement is a map, where do you want to go?

Where do you spend your time and energy?

What takes precedence in your life? Your job, family, faith, health, community, or something else?

How do you define your community?

Is it your family, colleagues, neighbors, friends near or far?

_____

_____

_____

_____

_____

_____

_____

How do you participate in your community?

_____

_____

_____

_____

_____

_____

_____

_____

_____

How do you serve your community?

....

....

....

....

....

....

....

....

Does that service bring you joy? In what ways do you use your skills
and talents to help others?

....

....

....

....

....

....

....

....

....

In 1988, acclaimed Black novelist Octavia Butler wrote herself a list of inspirational "I will" declarations. Alongside "I will write bestselling novels," she stated that she would help "Black youngsters" go to college and attend writing workshops.

When you achieve your vision, how will you give back?

Pick a single word that fits your vision.

My vision word:

What about that word speaks to you?

Explore your vision word here. Write it in different fonts, doodle about it, or collage images that remind you of it.

Body
Mind
Heart
Soul

48

BODY: What ideas give you energy and cause you to jump out of bed in the morning?

....

....

....

....

MIND: What do you continually think about doing, being, seeing, trying?

....

....

....

....

HEART: What bubbles in your heart?

....

....

....

....

SOUL: What is the core of your very being?

....

....

....

....

Time to Build Your Vision

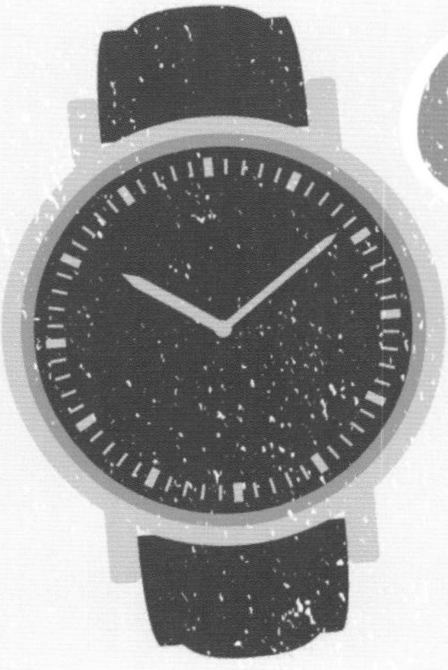

**BE MINDFUL.
MAKE TIME.**

CHAPTER 3

Putting Things into Action

Press Forward with a Plan

Now that you have a written vision, it's time to build your vision. Building requires a plan: step-by-step instructions that are not exhaustive, elaborate, or cumbersome. A plan that fits your identity and your behavior patterns.

According to the aphorism quoted many different ways by countless people: "Failing to plan is planning to fail." When you write it down, your plan keeps you focused even when you stumble upon obstacles or get sidetracked by detours along the way. Your plan may not guarantee success, but it will get you where you need to go and show you how to take the next logical step.

As you press forward, your plan helps you set boundaries that encourage productivity. When you set boundaries, you say "yes" to what is important. Instead of saying "I'm too busy," you learn to let folks around you know what you are doing: working on your goal, like finally landing an agent, purchasing a building for your bakery, returning to school, or taking time to rest and recover. This is the time to make an investment of your time. Since no plan is perfect, keep it simple, be flexible, and don't be afraid.

Sometimes plans change and need to be revamped. Flexibility makes your plan strong.

Your Habits and Preferences

Do you prefer winging it or planning it?

....

....

....

....

What are the benefits of your preferred method?

....

....

....

....

Have you ever tried the other method? Why, or why not?

....

....

....

....

Are you a list-maker or a schedule-builder?

....

....

....

....

....

....

Why does your method work better for you?

....

....

....

....

....

Have you ever tried the other method? Why, or why not?

....

....

....

....

....

....

Act on Your Plan

Put your plan into action.

Find a quiet space and take time to reflect. Your space should be free of distractions. If necessary, turn your phone off. Just put it away. It's time for you to think about things as you begin to make it happen.

Reread your vision statement on page 31. Your journey is your vision. Jot down some ideas you have for getting where you need to go.

How will you plan this journey? One step at a time, using a flow list that pushes your vision forward. With flow lists, you cannot linger too long on any one thing. Your idea is bubbling and brewing with things to do, people to see, and places to go. Pick up your pen and quickly empty your thoughts onto the page.

To start, write down everything that seems necessary. People who can help you and keep you accountable, events to attend, tasks to complete, and books to read.

Press forward.

Do not stop, do not linger in your journey, but strive for the mark set before you.

–George Whitefield

Next, build your vision house:

- In the triangle (the roof), write your vision.
- In each of the squares (the rooms of the house), write one goal that points to your vision. Now you have one vision and three goals.

Look at the goals you wrote on page 59. Below, come up with a to-do list for each goal. Refer to what you wrote on pages 56-58 for ideas.

The to-do lists flow together, creating a flow list.

Goal 1:

To-do:

Goal 2:

To-do:

_____

_____

_____

_____

_____

_____

Goal 3:

To-do:

_____

_____

_____

_____

_____

_____

_____

Now, expand on your to-do lists, and break them down into the categories on the following pages. Start with:

People to See

- [ ]
- [ ]
- [ ]
- [ ]
- [ ]
- [ ]
- [ ]
- [ ]
- [ ]
- [ ]
- [ ]
- [ ]
- [ ]
- [ ]
- [ ]
- [ ]
- [ ]
- [ ]
- [ ]

Tasks to Complete

- [ ]
- [ ]
- [ ]
- [ ]
- [ ]
- [ ]
- [ ]
- [ ]
- [ ]
- [ ]
- [ ]
- [ ]
- [ ]
- [ ]
- [ ]
- [ ]
- [ ]
- [ ]
- [ ]
- [ ]
- [ ]

Things to Learn and Books to Read

- [ ]
- [ ]
- [ ]
- [ ]
- [ ]
- [ ]
- [ ]
- [ ]
- [ ]
- [ ]
- [ ]
- [ ]
- [ ]
- [ ]
- [ ]
- [ ]
- [ ]
- [ ]
- [ ]

Places to Go

- [ ]
- [ ]
- [ ]
- [ ]
- [ ]
- [ ]
- [ ]
- [ ]
- [ ]
- [ ]
- [ ]
- [ ]
- [ ]
- [ ]
- [ ]
- [ ]
- [ ]
- [ ]
- [ ]

Things to Think About

- [ ]
- [ ]
- [ ]
- [ ]
- [ ]
- [ ]
- [ ]
- [ ]
- [ ]
- [ ]
- [ ]
- [ ]
- [ ]
- [ ]
- [ ]
- [ ]
- [ ]
- [ ]
- [ ]
- [ ]

Someday, Maybe...

- [ ]
- [ ]
- [ ]
- [ ]
- [ ]
- [ ]
- [ ]
- [ ]
- [ ]
- [ ]
- [ ]
- [ ]
- [ ]
- [ ]
- [ ]
- [ ]
- [ ]
- [ ]
- [ ]
- [ ]

A Sense of Your Vision

You've been thinking, planning, and visualizing something new or something to be renewed. Let's explore your senses. What does your vision feel, taste, sound, smell, and look like?

Set a timer for twenty minutes and write.

• CHAPTER 4 •

Be Willing to Make Mistakes

Find Fearlessness

Fearlessness is not an innate virtue. You achieve it not by superhuman strength, but by building a tenacious spirit and a confident attitude. To be fearless means you do not give up when you bump into hurdles or blunder on the way.

Fearlessness does not mean you are not fearful. Everyone fears something. According to motivational speaker Les Brown, "Too many of us are not living our dreams because we are living our fear." Fear manifests itself in infinite ways: the fear of being average, the fear of living up to someone else's expectations, the fear of not living up to someone else's expectations, the fear of public speaking, the fear of completion, and even the fear of success. But when you face that fear despite the obstacles you encounter (and you will face difficulty along the way), you become fearless.

In the introduction to Michelle Kuo's memoir *Reading with Patrick*, an exploration of racial inequality and the power of literature, Kuo confesses to finding her fearless role models in books: W.E.B. Du Bois, Ralph Ellison, Richard Wright, Alice Walker, and Maya Angelou. From her quiet bedroom in Michigan, while reading "antiracist rhetoric," Kuo realized it was not enough to read and admire Black writers: "If your passion went unmatched by actions, you were just playing a role, demonstrating that you knew what to praise and what to reject."

Kuo is the daughter of Taiwanese immigrants, who told her "cautionary tales about Asians in America being cowed, killed, and then forgotten." Michelle's parents were determined to raise her awareness "that tragedy might be right around the corner," and that education could serve as a safety net, particularly in math. Nevertheless, Michelle decided to be fearless. She stopped "choosing the safe option." She worked at a homeless shelter. She dropped out of pre-med and majored in social and gender studies. Upon graduation, Michelle was recruited by Teach for America to teach in one of the poorest places in the country, the Mississippi Delta. Despite her parents' disapproval and fear, Michelle pressed forward and became fearless with grit.

How do we diminish the distance between us? Reading is one way to close that distance. It gives us a quiet universe that we can share together, that we can share in equally.

—Michelle Kuo

What would you call your greatest fear?

What fears are you confronting now in your life?

Do your fears keep you safe or keep you stuck?

Describe how it feels to be safe or stuck.

If you had no *fears*, what would your life look like?

Today is
the day.

Get grit. Don't quit.

How much grit do you think you've got?
Can you quit a thing that you like a lot?

–Edgar Albert Guest, *"On Quitting"*

What makes you fearless is your passion and grit. You finish projects and believe yourself a hard worker. You just don't quit. Do you have grit?

Edgar Albert Guest's poem "On Quitting" asks the reader about tackling "self-discipline." No one desires "to quit the things that you like to do." But it's possible to be "tempted" or "swayed." The speaker reminds the reader, "Don't boast of your grit till you've tried it out."

The poem examines your grit and passion with probing questions: Can you turn from your "joys," have you put yourself to the test, just how far will you go?

How much grit do you
think you've got?

Can you turn from joys
that you like a lot?

Have you ever tested
yourself to know

How far with yourself
your will can go?

If you want to know
if you have grit,

Just pick out a joy that
you like, and quit.

Use these pages to respond to the poet's question.

Answer honestly. Tell him if you have grit, the staying power to finish what you've started. Describe a time you had to steel yourself and stick with something, and succeeded or failed. In your letter, describe your joy. Can you turn from it? Have you tried to walk away from a dream that calls you by name? How far have you pushed yourself to make it happen? Be fearless, and conclude your letter with why you are willing to **make it happen.**

To be fearless takes courage.

You may think you're wasting your time. Even those around you may not understand why you've chosen to push against the grain. To do something different.

Other projects may distract you because they seem more fruitful. Your inner critic and negative voices may crowd your thoughts. Let's quiet those voices.

On the next page take five minutes to write down what the naysayers are saying. That includes your own negative self-talk.

The naysayers are saying...

Now, change the negative talk to positive self-talk that is courageous and fearless. Write yourself a love letter.

Dear Me,

I am

I will

I can

I can

I can

I deserve

I have

I plan to give

I can

I can

I can

Others need me because

I will

I have

I can

I am capable because

This is my time to

STOP.
SAVOR.
Celebrate.

Look back over the journey. What do you see? Does it make your heart sing?

How will you celebrate this moment of being fearless?

What has fearlessness taught you about yourself?

Get to your goal.

PAST VICTORIES BRING PRESENT CONFIDENCE.

CHAPTER 5

You Got This!

Trust Yourself

Which one comes first: trusting yourself or being fearless?

To be fearless, you must name your fears and let them go.
Did you do that? Review your list on page 73. How are you feeling
about those fears?

....

....

....

....

....

After processing your fears, did you do something fearless?
What was it, and how did it feel? If you haven't yet, that's okay.
What fearless action could you take now?

....

....

....

....

....

....

....

After you take fearless action, make time to recharge. Take a walk, read a book, watch a movie, get a massage. Do nothing for 15 minutes. Remember, every accomplishment is an achievement, even getting out of the bed in the morning.

Confronting your fears builds your trust in your own power. You can confidently look at yourself in the mirror and say, "I trust myself."

Try it on the next page: Draw yourself or paste a picture of yourself in the frame, and fill in your name.

I trust: ....

your name here

I GOT THIS.

I trust myself.

AIN'T NO STOPPING ME.

Trusting yourself...

is not about becoming invincible or erasing self-doubt. It's reclaiming the power that you surrender to your fear. As the international yoga teacher Adriene Mishler says, "It's about showing up on the mat."

To trust yourself, you must know yourself. As Aristotle is often credited with saying, "knowing thyself is the beginning of all wisdom." And when you begin to trust yourself, you make decisions that point to your identity, things that make you comfortable and productive.

One example: A college student started a six-month cooperative educational position, where she would apply what she'd learned in the classroom on the job. In preparation, she needed to decide her travel options: ride the bus or drive her car. She decided to drive. The commute by car was faster than traveling by bus. She also knew that getting up early for a short commute fit her lifestyle. She considered her success rate at prior jobs and realized that the closer she lived to work, the more likely she would get to work on time. She knew that part of herself. You must trust your inner self, your habits, and your values.

Don't go it alone. Get your cheerleaders onboard.

Think about the people in your circle. That person who encourages you along. That person who knows something about you that you don't know about yourself.

Make a list of the people you know are in your corner:

....

....

....

....

....

....

....

....

....

....

....

....

....

....

....

Who has shown up for you when you needed them?

Who gives great advice?

Who can you trust to tell it like it is?

Alone we can do so little; together we can do so much.

— Helen Keller

Yes I Can.

Surrender your resistance.

Where are you repeatedly getting stuck in your journey?

....

....

....

....

....

Why do you think that sticking point remains?

....

....

....

....

....

What can you do to get unstuck? Can one of the people you listed on pages 94-95 help?

....

....

....

....

....

When we exist at the core of ourselves, we're departing from how we normally exist. We're bringing the

heart, mind, body, and soul

into focus and being present with them in a particular way: doing it on purpose, doing it with unconditional acceptance, and doing it with deep attentiveness.

—Sue Monk Kidd

Before moving on to the next step, take ten minutes and reflect about where you are on the journey.

Now is a good moment to reread what you wrote in the earlier sections of this journal.

What treasures did you find when rereading what you've written down?

....

....

....

When we commit our observations to writing, we take what is inside of us and place it outside of us. We hold a piece of our life in our hands, where we look at the journey we've taken, meditate on choices we've made, and deepen our understanding of ourselves. Be gentle with yourself. It's okay to revise if the notes are messy, or if you skipped parts. Fill them in now. Did you skip anything, or struggle to complete anything? If so, how do you feel about those sections now?

....

....

....

....

....

....

....

....

....

....

Are you beginning to see the big picture?

If so, what does it look like? If not, what do you think is preventing the big picture from coming together?

Confidence is making it happen.

TRUST YOURSELF;
TURN TO YOUR OWN
INSTINCTS.
DARE TO DREAM,
NOT TO COMPARE.
SURRENDER YOUR
RESISTANCE.

An Invitation to Dream

Write an article about your future success for a magazine or newspaper. What happened? To whom did it happen? What was the purpose of this endeavor? Who does this benefit? What's the overall goal? Is it a good goal?

The smallest idea, like the smallest seed, will grow quickly.

Watch it grow.

· CHAPTER 6 ·

It's Happening!

Sprout Like a Seed

The smallest idea, like the smallest seed, will grow quickly.

The mustard seed is approximately as wide as a pencil point. But once you put that seed in the ground, it sprouts rapidly, and the mustard plant grows to many times the seed's size in a matter of days.

The seed of a giant sequoia tree, meanwhile, is about the size of an oat flake. Once planted, the sequoia grows two feet in height each year during its first 50 to 100 years. The world's largest living sequoia is a tree called "General Sherman," standing 274 feet high with a diameter of 27 feet.

Although these small seeds sprout rapidly, you can't control the growth, only cooperate with it. Growth then becomes a mystery, and comes in its own time, just like your idea sprouts from a written vision to a plan with steps and goals. Take, for example, the story of the Chinese bamboo tree. In the first year there are no visible signs of growth. It is not until the fifth year, after fertilization, water, sun, and care, that the tree shoots from the ground, growing 80 to 90 feet in the next six weeks.

It happens one step at a time. But remember: There is something beyond the control of the farmer, planter, or arborist that makes the plants really grow. They, like you and your idea, have to trust the growth process to make it happen. That means you follow the basic guidelines and invest in yourself, your idea, and your habits. And along the way, celebrate the growth. Because it's happening!

What's Sprouting?

New people.
New places.
New things.

A plant, like an idea, doesn't grow overnight. It takes time, hard work, struggle, and resilience for a plant to sprout. Your idea needs the same nurturing and care.

Have you planted your seed?

....

....

....

What did you plant? Describe it in detail. Can you see its potential?

....

....

....

....

....

....

....

....

....

....

....

....

....

Did it sprout into a seedling? Check out its growth. Is it budding, flowering, or ripening? How?

_____

_____

_____

_____

_____

_____

_____

_____

What about its environment? Is your idea being supported by people around you?

_____

_____

_____

_____

_____

_____

_____

_____

Who is supporting your seedling, and how?

Do you need more positivity in your environment? If so, what weeds do you need to get rid of?

Don't judge each day by the harvest you reap but by the seeds that you plant.

—Robert Louis Stevenson

Are you comparing your growth to someone else's?

Who or what are you comparing yourself to? Why?

Don't compare yourself to others—
it will only put a damper on your idea.
Be brave enough to do something
difficult or dangerous or silly. Do
something that you have no right to
do. That's when you dare to dream,
making a commitment to your vision.

Be who you is, and not who you ain't. Because if you ain't who you is, then you is who you ain't. And that ain't good!

—John Kerdiejus

Is It Sustainable?

If your vision involves a product, service, or business, are you connecting with a need? If your vision is individual, are you meeting your own needs?

Is your plan financially feasible?

What collaborative possibilities does your vision offer?

What are some practical things that could slow your progress? (Budget issues? Time constraints? Life events?)

Do you have any plans for coping with these hurdles? What are they?

What are some internal issues that could slow your progress?
(Fatigue? Burnout? Distractions?)

Do you have any plans for coping with these hurdles? What are they?

Which of the obstacles that might come up are within your control?

Which obstacles are completely outside your control?

Do you worry about or fixate on the things you can't control?
If so, how do you manage that worry?

GRANT ME THE

serenity

TO ACCEPT THE THINGS
I CANNOT CHANGE,

courage

TO CHANGE THE THINGS
I CAN, AND

wisdom

TO KNOW THE DIFFERENCE.

Serenity Prayer

Overall, does your progress feel sustainable?

....

....

Why, or why not?

....

....

....

....

....

....

....

....

....

....

....

....

....

....

....

....

Every step
is a success.

You should be proud that you've come this far. Get excited about the progress, goals achieved, tasks completed, meetings to come.

Write down all the things you have done so far. Pay attention to the details. Every step you have made is a success.

Your life will be a great and continuous unfolding.

—Cheryl Strayed

• CHAPTER 7 •

Making a Choice

Wait for It

Waiting is the hardest part. Waiting causes tension and anxiety, especially since we live in a culture of instant gratification. Fast food. Instant potatoes. Microwavable dinner. But waiting is essential. A baker waits for the dough to rise. A woman waits to birth a child. Students wait to graduate. A homeowner waits for a loan approval.

When you wait, you make a choice to pursue delayed gratification. Waiting is not passive. You haven't been twiddling your thumbs; you're hoping things happen. You've been making choices that change who you are, what you are doing. You've been changing your view of the circumstances. Seeing your goals come to fruition.

What would we miss if waiting were eliminated from life? The deepest love stories, for one thing. You cannot name one that is not filled with this strange but common mystery: Waiting is worked into the design of any true lover's life.

In the novel *Zorba the Greek*, Zorba recalls a morning when he wanted to know the future. He discovered a cocoon in the bark of a tree, and noticed that a butterfly was trying to emerge from the cocoon. He waited a while, then became impatient with the natural process of the butterfly's birth. Zorba breathed on the butterfly to warm it, and the process sped up before his eyes. The butterfly started to crawl out, but to Zorba's horror, its wings were folded back and crumpled. The butterfly fearlessly struggled, but could not make it, and died. He had forced the butterfly to emerge before its time. As he held the little body in his hands, he realized the terrible thing that he had done. He said, "We should not hurry, we should not be impatient, but we should confidently obey the eternal rhythm." Is that not what we all need to do in our own lives: Obey the eternal rhythm?

Yes, you have worked hard, rewritten your vision, looked over your plan, even revised a few times. You have set goals and checked off lists. You want to know what's next. It's only a matter of time before something happens.

If it delays, wait for it, it will surely come, it will not be late.

—Habakkuk 2:3

Waiting can be
productive.

Don't rush
the process.

It will come
right on time.

Waiting is a cooling-off process. The question is:
What are you waiting for?

Take ten minutes to write down what you are waiting for.

By letting go, it all gets done.

– **Lao Tzu**

Sometimes while you're waiting for one thing, you're working on something else.

Make a list of all that you've done! When you make a list of what you've done, you don't panic or feel as though you're lacking. Instead you become grateful to the process. You love yourself along the way. You don't rush. You learn to take one step at a time.

Life is going to give you just what you put in it. Put your whole

heart

in everything you do, and pray, then you can wait.

– Maya Angelou

How do you feel about waiting?

Are you able to find peace with waiting? Does it feel restful, or make you anxious?

Are you ever tempted to rush things?

How has rushing served you in the past? Are there times when it's worked out well, badly, or somewhere in the middle?

How do you distinguish between purposeful action and "keeping yourself busy"?

With love and patience, nothing is impossible.

– Dr. Daisaku Ikeda

REFLECT.

Remember.

Before & After

Look back over everything you have written since you started this book. Mark places where you had "aha" moments. Moments where you stopped, left pages blank, pressed forward, resisted, became fearless.

What moments stand out to you throughout the book, and why?

Where did you truly dare to dream, and where did you skim the surface?

Did you make a commitment to yourself, and write your vision?
Can you repeat it by memory? Say it aloud now. Write it down again.

> There are a thousand thoughts lying
> within a man that he does not know
> till he takes up the pen to write, so the
> heart is a secret even to him [or her]
> who has it in his own breast.

—WILLIAM MAKEPEACE THACKERAY

Remember to be gentle with yourself. Setting goals and pressing forward when faced with obstacles and distractions can slow you down. But look how far you've come. Take a moment to map out your journey. Fill in the statements on these pages.

I dared to dream about

....

....

....

I wrote a vision that stated

....

....

....

I pressed forward despite

....

....

....

I was able to be fearless because

_____

_____

_____

_____

I trusted myself regardless of

_____

_____

_____

_____

My vision sprouted like a seed because

_____

_____

_____

_____

While I waited for other things to happen, this happened:

_____

_____

_____

140

As you look back at what you have written in this **Make It Happen** journal, highlight the moments you developed grit, especially if you didn't realize you had grit. How did it make you feel? Would you do it again? These are the times you begin to trust yourself and develop confidence. It's a transformation. Write down that transformation by completing these sentences.

I went from this ....

to that ....

I discovered this about myself:

....

....

....

....

....

....

....

....

....

....

....

I would not do .... again,

but I would do ....

As you look back over your journal, take note of your habits.

What patterns do you see?

What were some positive patterns and habits?

What were some negative patterns and habits?

What are some ways you can nurture the positive patterns?

What are some ways you can redirect the negative patterns?

When you began to see things happening, what did you do?
Did you rush the process? Wait and become productive in another
area of your life?

What are you going to do now?

Exploration Pages

Use these pages to explore your journey, get unstuck, re-align with your vision, and make it happen. When you hit an obstacle, return to this section. Set a timer for twenty minutes and write freely. Note your feelings, your thoughts, your frustrations, your excitement. Let loose with your pen and see what ideas emerge.

What the caterpillar calls the end of the world, the master calls a butterfly.

—Richard Bach

**Persistence is critical.
Being creative and persistent is even better.**
—Katie Couric

At the center of your being you have the answer; you know who you are and you know what you want.

—M. J. Ryan

So keep moving forward. And don't be frustrated
when your path gets messy because it will get
messy. You'll fall and you'll fail along the way.
Wildly. Embrace the mess. . . . Get ready for it.
And don't let the potential to fail stop you
from moving forward.

—*Octavia Spencer*

*What you do makes a difference,
and you have to decide what kind of
difference you want to make.*

—Jane Goodall

You have to participate relentlessly in the manifestation of your own blessings.

—Elizabeth Gilbert

About the Author

Angela R. Hooks, Ph.D. is a diary keeper of over three decades. Using diaries, journals, and notebooks, she has realized and actualized several goals. As a writer, teacher, preacher, and speaker, she uses an interdisciplinary approach that blends writing, literature, religion, and the arts together, appealing to head and heart.